P9-CMW-598

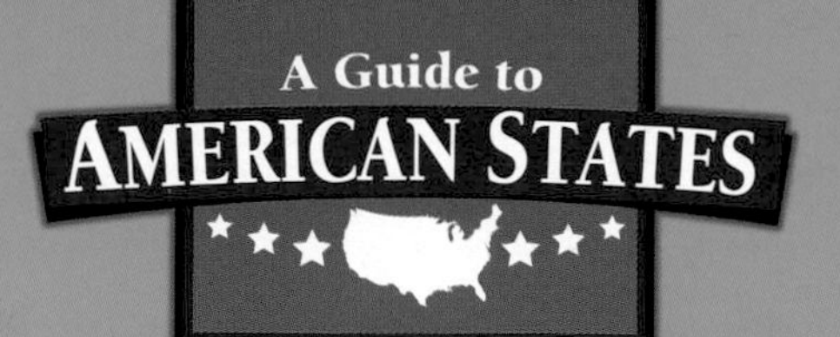

South Carolina

THE PALMETTO STATE

www.av2books.com

Go to www.av2books.com, and enter this book's unique code.

AV^2 by Weigl brings you media enhanced books that support active learning.

AV^2 provides enriched content that supplements and complements this book. Weigl's AV^2 books strive to create inspired learning and engage young minds in a total learning experience.

Your AV^2 Media Enhanced books come alive with...

Audio
Listen to sections of the book read aloud.

Key Words
Study vocabulary, and complete a matching word activity.

Video
Watch informative video clips.

Quizzes
Test your knowledge.

Embedded Weblinks
Gain additional information for research.

Slide Show
View images and captions, and prepare a presentation.

Try This!
Complete activities and hands-on experiments.

... and much, much more!

Published by AV^2 by Weigl
350 5th Avenue, 59th Floor
New York, NY 10118
Website: www.av2books.com www.weigl.com

Library of Congress Cataloging-in-Publication Data

Parker, Janice.
South Carolina / Janice Parker.
p. cm. -- (A guide to American states)
Includes index.
ISBN 978-1-61690-813-3 (hardcover : alk. paper) -- ISBN 978-1-61690-489-0 (online)
1. South Carolina--Juvenile literature. I. Title.
F269.3.P373 2011
975.7--dc23
2011019032

Printed in the United States of America in North Mankato, Minnesota

052011
WEP180511

Project Coordinator Jordan McGill
Art Director Terry Paulhus

Photo Credits
Every reasonable effort has been made to trace ownership and to obtain permission to reprint copyright material. The publishers would be pleased to have any errors or omissions brought to their attention so that they may be corrected in subsequent printings.

Weigl acknowledges Getty Images as its primary image supplier for this title.

Contents

Brilliant flowers and native plants thrive in South Carolina's elegant historic gardens.

Introduction

South Carolina is a state to celebrate. And South Carolinians have the festivals to prove it. They celebrate their food with the Lowcountry Shrimp Festival, the Peanut Party in Pelion, and the Watermelon Festival in Hampton. They rejoice in the natural beauty of their state with separate festivals for roses and irises, as well as the South Carolina Festival of Flowers in Greenwood. They honor their history by preserving numerous American Revolution and Civil War battlefields. South Carolinians also stage dramatic re-creations of the Civil War's Battle of Aiken and other battles.

Whitewater rafting on South Carolina's many rivers provides thrills to the adventurous.

Myrtle Beach is one of the nation's top vacation spots, luring millions of visitors annually to its white-sand beaches.

As one of the original 13 colonies that formed the United States, the state has a long, fascinating history. The smallest state in the Deep South, South Carolina has a varied landscape and a warm climate. With its friendly residents and natural beauty, including mountains and seashores, the state also boasts a booming tourist industry. Hilton Head, an island off the coast of South Carolina, attracts well over 2 million tourists every year. They come for the more than 24 championship golf courses. They enjoy the quiet beauty of nature preserves, such as Sea Pines Forest Preserve and Audubon-Newhall Preserve. The alligators, herons, and kingfishers living in the lagoons also draw visitors. So does the local food based on seafood, pork barbecue, and other Southern dishes.

Once based primarily on agriculture, the economy of South Carolina gradually moved toward an industrial base. Today manufacturing is one of the most significant industries in South Carolina. However, most South Carolinians work in the service sector, which includes retail sales, health care, government, and tourism.

Where Is South Carolina?

South Carolina is shaped like a triangle. The state is bordered by North Carolina to the north and northeast, Georgia to the west and southwest, and the Atlantic Ocean to the east and southeast. South Carolina's land area of 30,109 square miles makes it the 11th smallest state in the nation.

English settlers established a colony in South Carolina in the late 1600s. Many of the colonists owned **plantations** and grew crops such as rice and cotton. They used slaves from Africa to work in the fields. During the mid-1800s, a dispute between the Northern and Southern states arose over the issue of slavery. While much of the North opposed slavery, the South wanted to keep its slaves and plantation culture. On December 20, 1860, South Carolina became the first state to **secede** from the United States, or the Union. It became part of the rebellious Confederate States of America.

At the start of the Civil War, Confederate cannons pounded Fort Sumter for 30 hours until the Union fort's commander was forced to surrender.

The Civil War began on April 12, 1861, when Confederate troops fired upon Fort Sumter in Charleston Harbor. During the war, South Carolina's coast was the site of much fighting. After the Confederacy was defeated, the state was readmitted to the Union. It began to rebuild its economy. New industries, such as textiles, helped pave the way to a brighter future.

Today buildings that date back to before the Civil War can still be seen in such cities as Beaufort and Charleston. Large plantations also still exist in parts of South Carolina. The state's beautiful gardens, blooming with flowers such as magnolias, are fragrant reminders of the natural landscape of colonial times in South Carolina.

By 1730, slaves brought from Africa and their descendants made up about two-thirds of the population of the South Carolina colony.

I DIDN'T KNOW THAT!

South Carolina is called the Palmetto State, named for the distinctive tree that grows along the state's coast.

The state flag is based on one created in 1775 during the American Revolution by Colonel William Moultrie for his troops. His flag featured a crescent, which represented the silver emblems on the soldiers' caps. Later a palmetto tree was added to the center of the flag to represent the brave defense of the palmetto-log fort on Sullivan's Island by Moultrie and his troops.

South Carolina is in the Eastern time zone. The state observes daylight saving time from early March to early November.

The Columbia Metropolitan Airport is the state's largest airport, covering some 2,600 acres.

The state was the site of many battles during the American Revolution. The British captured the city of Charleston in 1780.

About one-fourth of the 63,000 soldiers from South Carolina who fought in the Civil War were killed during the war.

Mapping South Carolina

Visitors can get to the state in a variety of ways, but air travel is often the fastest mode of transportation. South Carolina has four major airports. For automobile travelers, South Carolina has about 64,000 miles of roads, two-thirds of which are maintained by the state. Railroads provide freight service and also allow for passenger trains.

Sites and Symbols

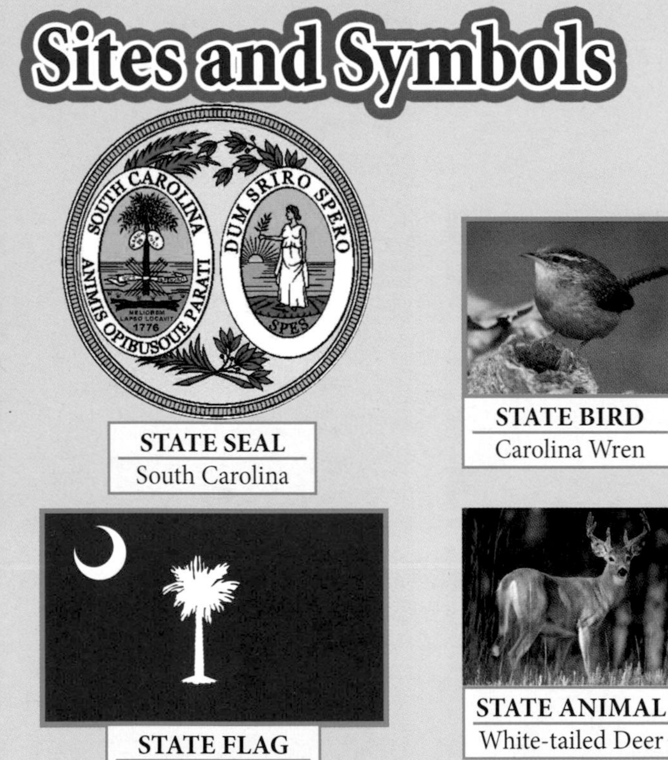

STATE SEAL
South Carolina

STATE BIRD
Carolina Wren

STATE FLOWER
Yellow Jessamine

STATE FLAG
South Carolina

STATE ANIMAL
White-tailed Deer

STATE TREE
Cabbage Palmetto

Nickname The Palmetto State

Motto *Animis Opibusque Parati* (Prepared in Mind and Resources) and *Dum Spiro Spero* (While I Breathe, I Hope)

Song "Carolina," words by Henry Timrod and music by Anne Custis Burgess, and "South Carolina on My Mind," words and music by Hank Martin and Buzz Arledge

Entered the Union May 23, 1788, as the 8th state

Capital Columbia

Population (2010 Census) 4,625,364 Ranked 24th state

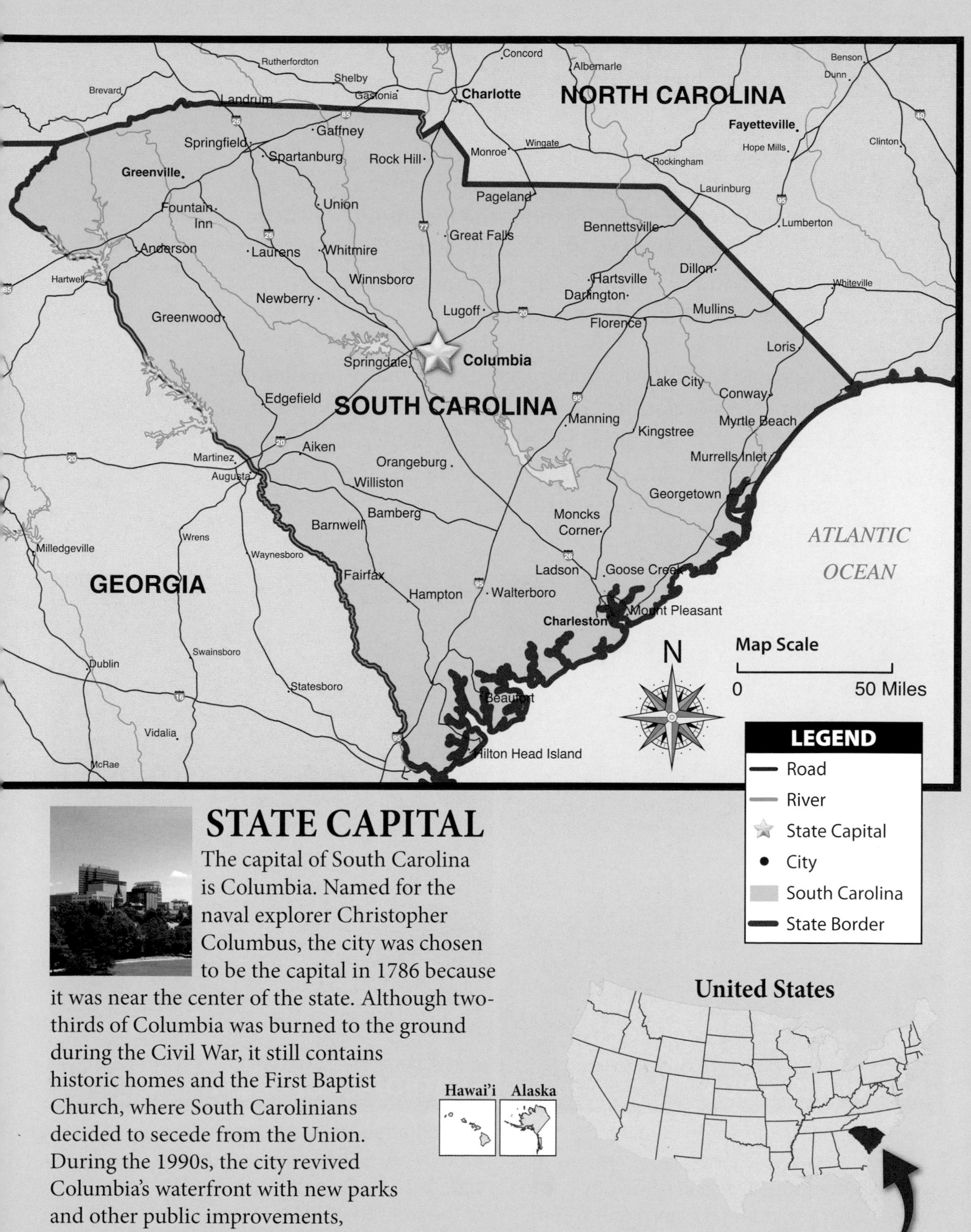

STATE CAPITAL

The capital of South Carolina is Columbia. Named for the naval explorer Christopher Columbus, the city was chosen to be the capital in 1786 because it was near the center of the state. Although two-thirds of Columbia was burned to the ground during the Civil War, it still contains historic homes and the First Baptist Church, where South Carolinians decided to secede from the Union. During the 1990s, the city revived Columbia's waterfront with new parks and other public improvements, attracting new businesses and shops.

The Land

South Carolina has three distinct land regions. The low-lying Atlantic Coastal Plain in the southern and eastern parts of the state is mainly flat. Farther inland is the Piedmont, a plateau with rolling hills that covers about one-third of the state. The Blue Ridge region is a tiny area in the northwestern portion of the state. It is dominated by the Blue Ridge Mountains.

South Carolina also includes 13 major islands and many smaller ones. The three main rivers of South Carolina are the Santee, Savannah, and Great Pee Dee rivers. At 143 miles in length, the Santee is the longest river that falls entirely within the state. There are no large natural lakes in South Carolina, but many artificial ones have been created by damming the major rivers.

BARRIER ISLANDS

Barrier islands lie off South Carolina's eastern coast. These long islands are typically composed of sand carried by ocean waves. Beaches, dunes, swampy areas, and different kinds of plants cover the islands.

SUBTROPICAL FOREST

Moss-draped live oaks, magnolia trees, loblolly pines, holly trees, southern red cedars, and wild palmettos are just a few of the trees that thrive in the subtropical forests of South Carolina.

ACE BASIN

The ACE Basin, named after the Ashepoo, Combahee, and Edistor rivers, is a protected area of marshes, wetlands, forests, and rivers. Once used for growing rice, the area gradually became primarily hunting land. A combination of government and private funding has helped preserve much of the area in its natural state.

BLUE RIDGE MOUNTAINS

Part of the Appalachian Mountain chain, the Blue Ridge Mountains form a narrow ridge. It ranges from 5 to 65 miles wide and from 2,000 to 4,000 feet high. The mountains get their name from the blue haze that often wraps around the peaks.

I DIDN'T KNOW THAT!

At 3,560 feet, Sassafras Mountain is the highest point in South Carolina.

South Carolinians call the eastern part of the state the "Low Country" while the western part is known as the "Up Country."

South Carolina's Atlantic coastline is approximately 187 miles long. But if all the bays, inlets, and islands are included, the state has 2,876 miles of coastline.

The Grand Strand is a 60-mile stretch of white-sand beach that runs along the South Carolina coast from Little River to Georgetown.

Hundreds of "Carolina bays" are scattered on the state's Atlantic Coastal Plain. Swamp plants surround water in the middle of these oval depressions. No one knows for sure what caused these basin-like formations. However, some scientists think that comets or meteors may have struck Earth, causing these hollows.

South Carolina's warm climate allows many kinds of subtropical plants and trees to flourish. The growing season ranges from nearly 200 days in the northwest to about 290 days on the Sea Islands off the southeastern coast.

South Carolina has a subtropical climate with hot, humid summers and mild winters. Average January temperatures in South Carolina range from about 40° to 50° Fahrenheit. In July, most of the state has an average temperature of about 80° F, except in the mountains, where temperatures average around 70° F.

An average of 10 tornadoes touch down in South Carolina every year, usually in spring. Hurricanes sometimes hit coastal areas.

Average Annual Precipitation Across South Carolina

Cities in various parts of South Carolina typically receive somewhat different amounts of rainfall over the course of a year, but the differences are not very large. What might account for the relative uniformity of rainfall across the state?

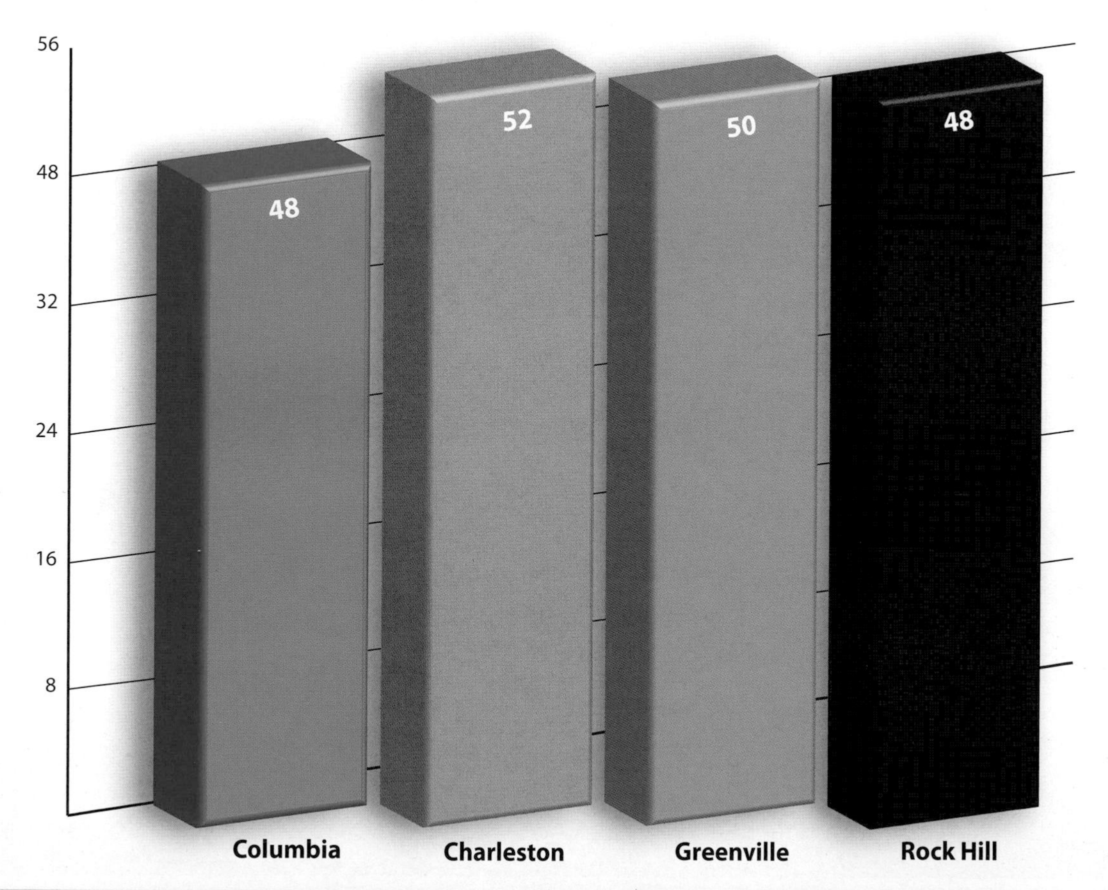

Natural Resources

Natural resources in South Carolina include vast forests, rich soils, minerals, and a plentiful water supply. About two-thirds of South Carolina is forested. Almost three-fourths of the forests in the state are privately owned.

Many minerals used in construction and other industries are mined in South Carolina, including clay, granite, limestone, and vermiculite. A lightweight material, vermiculite is used in potting soil and insulation, as well as to incubate eggs or grow fungi.

Limestone is used in fertilizers and also in buildings for floors and walls.

South Carolina is among the nation's top producers of kaolin, a soft, white clay. There were about 30 kaolin mines in the state in the early 21st century. Kaolin is used in many products, including paper, tires, paint, and cosmetics.

Limestone was first mined in South Carolina in the 1820s. It is one of the main ingredients of portland cement, which is a binding material. South Carolina produces a great deal of portland cement each year.

South Carolina's beaches, swamps, mountain forests, and nature preserves are also a natural resource. They attract millions of tourists every year.

South Carolina's beautiful lakes and rivers attract tourists for kayaking, canoeing, sailing, and other water sports.

I DIDN'T KNOW THAT!

Gold was mined near the town of Ridgeway from 1988 to 1990. While the mine was operational, it was the only mine producing gold east of the Mississippi River. The area is now being reclaimed for recreational use.

Vermiculite is a mineral that expands to 20 times its size when it is heated. The state is one of the leading producers of this mineral in the country.

Granite is a rock that is used primarily in the construction industry. It was first mined in South Carolina in about 1786.

Plants

Considering its small size, South Carolina has a large variety of plants. Loblolly and longleaf pine trees are common throughout the state's forests. Other trees include oak, cypress, magnolia, elm, sycamore, and tupelo. White pine and hemlock grow throughout the woodlands of the Pine Ridge. In the Piedmont area, vast forests of loblolly pines have replaced worn-out farmland.

Cattails and bulrushes sway in the freshwater marshes along the coast, while cordgrass, black rushes, glasswort, and sea ox-eye flourish in the saltwater marshes. The state tree, the cabbage palmetto, also grows along the coast.

Flowering shrubs and wildflowers grow throughout the state, including flowering dogwood and yellow jessamine, or jasmine. Mountain laurel and various types of rhododendron thrive in the mountain regions.

KUDZU

Kudzu can grow up to one foot every day. People used to plant it to control **erosion**. Now it has become a pest, covering and killing plants by blocking the sunlight they need to grow.

CABBAGE PALMETTO

An evergreen palm tree, the cabbage palmetto can grow as tall as 33 feet. Its leaves can be as large as 3 feet across. Raccoons, robins, and other birds feed on the tree's fruit. People use its big leaf bud in salads, pickles, and relishes.

VENUS FLYTRAP

Each leaf of this rare plant is hinged at the middle. This feature allows it to snap shut around any insect or spider that lands on it. The plant's sap then digests its prey.

SEA OATS

These grasses thrive in sandy areas and can grow to 6 feet tall. They trap windblown sand that eventually forms into dunes. Sea oats also tolerate salt water, making them excellent beach cover for protecting coastlines from erosion.

I DIDN'T KNOW THAT!

The yellow jessamine became the official state flower in 1924. The flower had long been a favorite of South Carolinians.

South Carolina and North Carolina are perhaps the only places in the world where the Venus flytrap grows wild.

Pitcher plants grow wild in South Carolina. They have hooded, pitcher-shaped leaves that trap insects.

South Carolina is one of the largest producers of peaches in the country.

Goldenrod is the official state wildflower. Goldenrod blooms in late summer and early fall. Its bright yellow flowers grow in fields, meadows, and along roadsides throughout the state.

Animals

Common wild animals in the state include the white-tailed deer, beavers, and squirrels. Hundreds of species of birds have been spotted in South Carolina. Hawks, owls, wild turkeys, and bald eagles live in the state. Other native birds include the swallow, Baltimore oriole, and pelican. South Carolina's coast is part of the Atlantic Flyway, a north-south route used by many species of birds during their annual migration.

Turtles, lizards, salamanders, frogs, and toads can be found in South Carolina's swamps. Dolphins swim offshore. The largest reptile in North America, the American alligator, lives in the lakes, streams, and swamps of the state's Atlantic Coastal Plain. The American alligator can be as long as 20 feet. It is black with bands of yellow that fade with age. This alligator can be dangerous to humans.

WHITE-TAILED DEER

The white-tailed deer is the oldest living species of deer in the world. Adult deer coats are reddish brown in summer and grayish brown in winter. Fawns, or baby deer, are spotted. This coloring helps them blend in with the forest floor to hide from predators.

LOGGERHEAD TURTLE

The shell of an adult loggerhead turtle can grow to 3 or 4 feet long. These sea turtles have huge jaws to crush clamshells. They appear on land only to lay their eggs in the sand.

BOTTLENOSE DOLPHIN

Graceful, friendly, and intelligent, bottlenose dolphins communicate with clicks, squeals, and whistles. Speedy swimmers, these toothed whales can reach almost 18 miles per hour in short bursts.

WILD TURKEY

A wild turkey's head is normally red but turns white and bright blue when it is excited. A wattle hangs from its throat. Male turkeys can weigh up to 22 pounds, while females are much smaller.

I DIDN'T KNOW THAT!

South Carolina has many official kinds of wildlife besides the state animal. The striped bass is the state fish, the loggerhead turtle is the state reptile, the spotted salamander is the state amphibian, the Carolina mantid is the state insect, and the Eastern tiger swallowtail is the state butterfly. The Boykin Spaniel, which is the official state dog of South Carolina, was first bred in the state as a hunting dog.

European settlers brought the wild pig and the red fox to South Carolina.

South Carolina is home to dozens of snake species, including some poisonous snakes.

The coastal waters are home to fish such as sea trout, shad, and barracuda. Trout, striped bass, largemouth bass, catfish, and pickerel are found in freshwater streams and lakes.

Tourism

Known for its warm climate, lush mountains, long coastline, and friendly people, South Carolina is a popular tourist destination. In fact, an average of 28.5 million people traveled to South Carolina each year during the late 2000s. Many came to explore the Grand Strand area, which enjoys more than 200 sunny days each year. Myrtle Beach is located along the Grand Strand.

Many other attractions draw visitors to the state. South Carolina's lakes attract families for fishing, waterskiing, kayaking, and canoeing. Some people visit the mountains to hike and explore nature. Others ride the roller coasters at the state's many amusement parks. History buffs travel to Charleston, where they can tour buildings from the colonial period. Charleston also has many museums, including the Confederate Museum, which displays Confederate army uniforms and equipment.

MYRTLE BEACH

Amusement parks are among the many attractions of Myrtle Beach. Ferris wheels carry riders to great heights, allowing them to look over the parks and cities below. Myrtle Beach Pavilion Amusement Park boasts the state's largest wooden roller coaster and an arcade along the ocean.

HILTON HEAD

While serious golfers may flock to Hilton Head for the championship courses, miniature golf attracts families and players of all ages. Visitors can also explore charming small towns or go shell hunting on the island's gorgeous beaches.

FORT SUMTER

Fort Sumter was built on an artificial island in Charleston's harbor. Enduring four years of cannon fire during the Civil War, much of the fort was completely destroyed. Today the Fort Sumter National Monument includes a partially rebuilt fort and a museum with historical displays.

MAGNOLIA PLANTATION AND GARDENS

The Magnolia Plantation and Gardens is on the site of a large farm that was founded in Charleston in 1676. It features the Barbados Tropical Garden, the oldest public garden in the United States.

I DIDN'T KNOW THAT!

South Carolina has two national forests, Sumter and Francis Marion, and 47 state parks.

The American Military Museum in Charleston has exhibits on the major wars involving the Unites States.

The historic submarine *H.L. Hunley* is on display in Charleston. In 1864, during the Civil War, this Confederate vessel became the first submarine to sink an enemy ship. After its mission, the *Hunley* mysteriously sank in the harbor. It was not discovered until 1995.

Hilton Head Island has several large tourist resorts. With an area of 42 square miles, it is the largest island of South Carolina. People visit Hilton Head to play golf and tennis, swim, and enjoy the beaches.

Agriculture was the backbone of South Carolina's economy through the early 1900s. Although agriculture is still important to the state more than a century later, many more South Carolinians now work in service and manufacturing industries. Manufacturing focuses on textiles, industrial machinery, and chemicals.

Industries in South Carolina

Value of Goods and Services in Millions of Dollars

South Carolina once relied on agriculture to support its economy. However, tourism has become one of the fastest-growing sources of income in the state. What industries thrive to a large extent by meeting the needs of tourists?

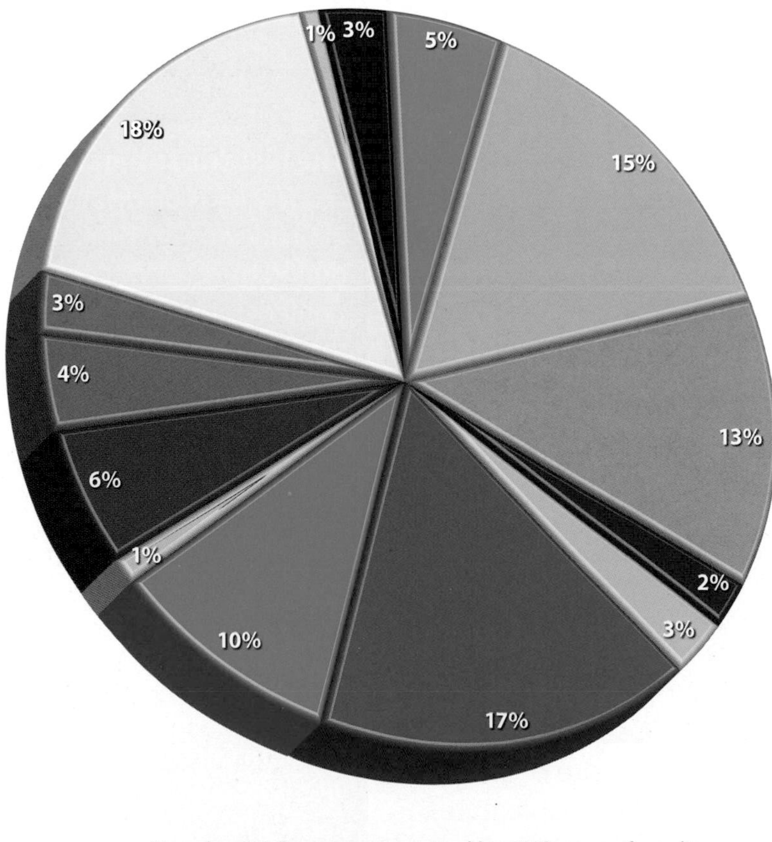

*Less than 1%. Percentages may not add to 100 because of rounding.

LEGEND

Industry	Value
Agriculture, Forestry, and Fishing	$1,062
* Mining	$281
Utilities	$4,563
Construction	$7,557
Manufacturing	$24,109
Wholesale and Retail Trade	$20,530
Transportation	$3,546
Media and Entertainment	$5,340
Finance, Insurance, and Real Estate	$27,403
Professional and Technical Services	$15,182
Education	$1,058
Health Care	$10,031
Hotels and Restaurants	$5,883
Other Services	$4,534
Government	$28,568
TOTAL	**$159,647**

One of the state's leading agricultural products is broiler chickens, which are chickens raised for eating, not for producing eggs. Turkeys, cattle, cotton, soybeans, tomatoes, and peanuts are also important agricultural products.

South Carolina is one of the largest producers in the nation of peaches and flue-cured tobacco. Flue-cured tobacco is dried by artificial heat rather than hung in barns to air-dry. Tobacco, grown primarily in the Pee Dee region, accounts for nearly one-fourth of all income earned from crops in South Carolina.

Much of South Carolina is forested, almost 13 million acres. About 3.1 million acres are planted in pine forest, and 2.8 million acres are covered in natural pine forest. Oaks and other hardwood trees make up much of the other forestland. The state produces about $1 billion in forest products, including paper products and wood for construction.

South Carolina is one of the top three peach-producing states in the nation. Peach orchards, with their beautiful pink blossoms in the spring, grow on about 18,000 acres of the state's farmland.

In 2009, there were about 27,000 farms in South Carolina.

The boll weevil, a type of beetle, damaged many cotton crops in South Carolina during the 1920s. As a result, farmers began raising other crops, such as fruit, tobacco, and wheat.

Shrimp, crabs, clams, and oysters are among the most important commercial products of the state's fishing industry.

The peach is the state fruit of South Carolina.

The loblolly pine grows to maturity and can be harvested for its wood in only 20 years.

Goods and Services

Chemicals are the leading manufactured products in South Carolina. The main products in this category include plastic resins, dyes, and medicines. The major centers for chemical production are the cities of Greenville, Spartanburg, Columbia, and Aiken.

The production of textiles, or cloth, fibers, and yarn, has a long and important economic history in the state. Even though many textile-manufacturing facilities were moved overseas in the late 20th century, many South Carolinians are still employed by textile companies. Milliken & Company, which is headquartered in Spartanburg, is one of the nation's largest textile firms. The company has a large textile research center and holds more than 2,300 **patents** in the United States alone. Mount Vernon Mills, Inc., a textile company based in Mauldin, is another of the country's leading textile firms. The company dates back to the 1840s.

Cotton fabrics are the state's most significant textile product, but South Carolina also produces yarn, carpets, and synthetic fibers, such as nylon and rayon.

South Carolina is home to drug manufacturers as well as many research institutes focused on developing new medicines.

Sonoco, a company with headquarters in Hartsville, is one of the world's largest producers of packaging materials, such as plastic bags. The company is also one of the leading producers of recycled cardboard.

Greenville is the home of Michelin's North American headquarters. Michelin, based in France, manufactures tires.

About half of the electricity produced in South Carolina is generated by nuclear power plants. The state has four nuclear power plants with a total of seven reactors. Much of the remainder of the state's electricity comes from coal-fueled power plants.

South Carolina has been working to improve its education system. The state passed laws in 1984 and 1998 to raise learning standards and to provide increased funding for education.

In the late 1920s, South Carolina billed itself as the Iodine State. The state was promoting the health benefits of crops grown in the state's iodine-rich soil.

Nearly 10 percent of South Carolina's workforce is employed in the tourism industry. In addition to tourism, service industries in the state employing many workers include government, retail and wholesale businesses, health-care facilities, financial services companies, and firms providing other business services.

South Carolina has numerous facilities for higher education. The University of South Carolina, which was chartered in 1801, educates more than 44,000 students on its eight campuses. It offers about 320 degree programs for its students.

American Indians

American Indians have lived in the South Carolina region for more than 10,000 years. In about 2000 BC, they began to plant crops such as corn and squash. About 900 years ago, a group called the Mound Builders flourished in the area.

Much later, in the 1600s, about 30 different groups of American Indians lived in the South Carolina region. They had a total population of about 15,000. Two groups who lived in the northern and western parts of the region were the Cherokee and the Catawba. Unlike many other tribes in the Southeast who spoke Muskogean languages, the Cherokees spoke an Iroquoian language. They lived in villages with homes made from small trees, mud, and bark.

Traditional Cherokee homes were built of branches held together with mud.

The Catawbas spoke a Siouan language and were known for their tradition of making pottery. Early Catawba potters worked with clay that was sometimes mixed with Spanish moss. They often rolled the clay into coils, which they then formed into bowls. They wore clothes of deerskin, and in the winter, they added capes and leggings made of other animal skins. Their jewelry was made of shells, beads, and copper.

Today the largest American Indian group in South Carolina is the Pee Dee. The ancestors of the Pee Dees raised squash, corn, and beans and gathered nuts, berries, and other fruits. Most Pee Dees today live in the northeast.

Modern-day American Indians sometimes dress in ceremonial clothing for powwows, or celebrations of Indian culture. Traditional Cherokee clothing is made of deerskin.

I DIDN'T KNOW THAT!

During 1838 and 1839, many thousands of Cherokees in the southeastern states were forced at gunpoint or bayonet point to leave their homes and travel on foot to what is now Oklahoma. U.S. soldiers grabbed children while their parents were working in the fields, thus making sure the parents would follow. During this march, called the Trail of Tears, some 4,000 Cherokees died.

Many Catawba live on a reservation near Rock Hill. In 1993, the United States government officially recognized the Catawba's land claims. They were given $50 million and 144,000 acres of land in York County.

In traditional Cherokee culture, members follow the "Harmony Ethic." This code discourages people from displaying anger and encourages sharing, especially of food. It emphasizes reducing conflict between individuals.

For thousands of years, Cherokee women have been weaving baskets to store goods, food, fish, and small game. The baskets were made from cane, white oak, hickory bark, and honeysuckle.

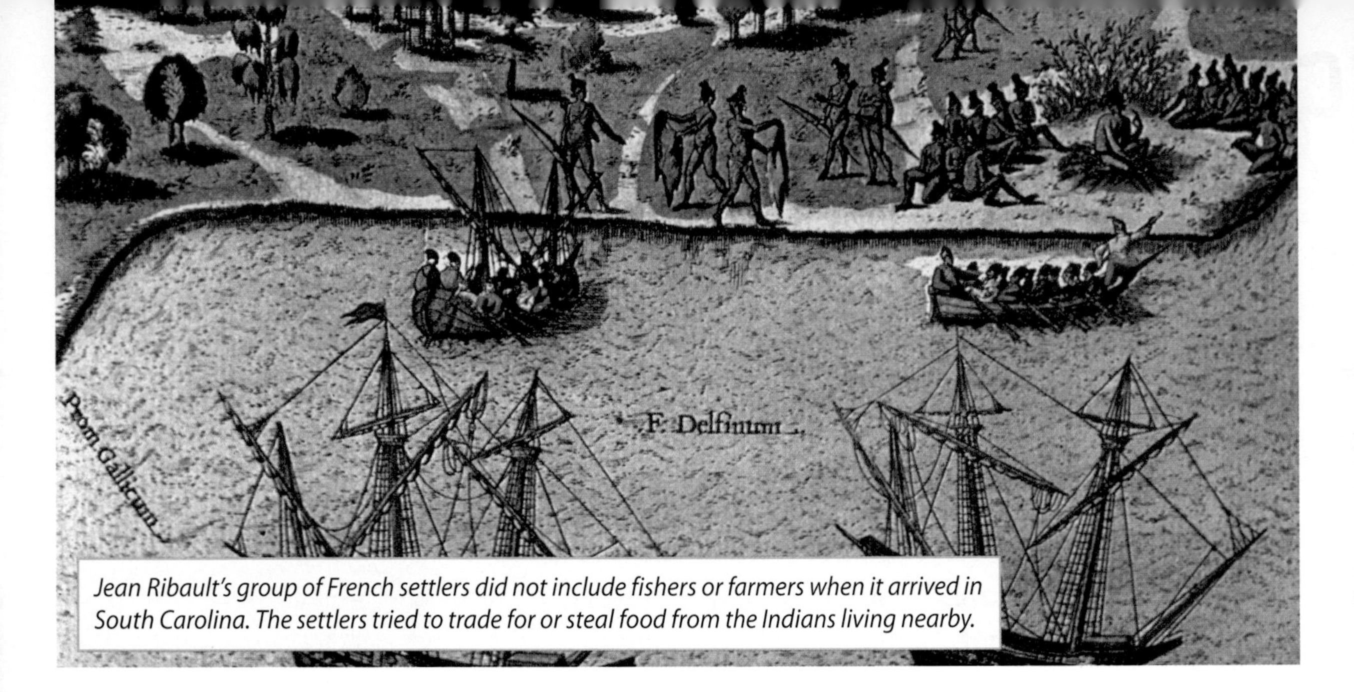

Jean Ribault's group of French settlers did not include fishers or farmers when it arrived in South Carolina. The settlers tried to trade for or steal food from the Indians living nearby.

Explorers

In 1521, Francisco Gordillo led a Spanish expedition that explored the coast of what is now South Carolina. He stopped to trade goods with the American Indians along the coast. When he left, he took more than 100 Indians with him as slaves.

Lucas Vásquez de Ayllón, another Spanish explorer, came to the area in 1526 with about 600 people. He started a colony near present-day Georgetown. The colony faced many difficulties. Illness, problems with the Americans Indians, and bad weather forced the group to travel home after just a few months.

In 1562, the French tried unsuccessfully to start a colony on Parris Island. Captain Jean Ribaut and a small group of French Huguenots built a fort there. The Huguenots were Protestants who left France to escape religious **persecution**. Soon after they arrived, Ribaut sailed back to France to get more men and supplies. He did not return, however, and the Huguenots soon abandoned the settlement. A few years later, a group of Spanish settlers established a colony on the island at Santa Elena. However, in 1587, the town and fort were abandoned as the Spanish withdrew from the area.

Timeline of Settlement

Early Exploration

1521 Francisco Gordillo from Spain leads an expedition that explores what is now South Carolina.

1526 Spanish explorer Lucas Vásquez de Ayllón tries to establish a colony, which ultimately fails due to disease and other factors.

1562 French Huguenots led by Captain Jean Ribaut build a fort on Parris Island.

European Settlements and Control

1670 English lord Anthony Ashley Cooper starts a small colony at Albemarle Point, the first permanent European settlement in South Carolina. The colony later moves to what will become the site of Charleston.

1719 Carolina, consisting of present-day North and South Carolina, becomes a separate royal province ruled by the British.

1729 The British split the province into North and South Carolina.

Independence and Statehood

1776 South Carolina joins 12 other British colonies in declaring their independence. The Americans win two major victories against the British in South Carolina, at the battle of Kings Mountain in 1780 and the battle of Cowpens in 1781.

1783 After the American Revolution, Great Britain formally recognizes the independence of the United States, which includes South Carolina.

1788 South Carolina becomes the 8th state on May 23.

Civil War and Reunification

1860 South Carolina secedes from the Union.

1861–1865 South Carolina fights on the side of the Confederacy in the Civil War. After four years of war, the Confederacy is defeated.

1868 South Carolina is readmitted to the Union as a state.

In 1629, King Charles I of England granted parts of North America to Sir Robert Heath. This area included a strip of land containing what are now the states of South Carolina and North Carolina. The English did not immediately colonize the area, however.

Map of Settlements and Resources in Early South Carolina

❶ English settlers establish a colony on Albemarle Point in 1670. They trade with local Indians and export deerskins.

❷ During the 1700s, English settlers discover that rice grows well in the inland valley swamps of the Low Country.

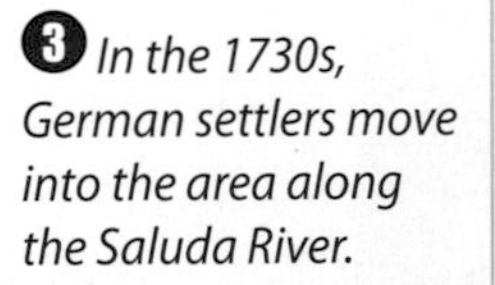

❹ In 1735, about 250 Swiss people establish a town now called Orangeburg.

❺ During the 1750s and 1760s, Scotch-Irish settlers from the colonies of Pennsylvania and Virginia move into the South Carolina Piedmont area, where they take advantage of the region's good farmland.

❻ Gold is discovered for the first time in South Carolina in 1802, in the Greenville area.

N

Scale

0 50 Miles

LEGEND

Settlement
River
Farming
Rice
Gold
South Carolina
State Border

In 1663, King Charles II granted the land to eight other English noblemen, and they sent settlers there. In 1670, nearly 150 colonists created the first permanent European settlement in what is now South Carolina. Many of the colonists had been living on the island of Barbados. They called their new settlement Charles Town. Ten years later, the settlement was moved across the river to a better location, the site of present-day Charleston.

Some 5,000 people had settled in the area by 1700. The population included some French Huguenots, who came from New England. In 1729, Carolina was split into North Carolina and South Carolina. By the following year, South Carolina was home to about 30,000 settlers, who lived mostly in or around Charles Town.

During the mid-1700s, a rivalry began between people living in two different areas of South Carolina. These areas were the Low Country, or the low-lying land of the coastal plain including Charles Town, and the Up Country, which was farther inland and higher in elevation. Low Country residents were often wealthy plantation owners. Much of their land was cultivated by black Africans who were made to work as slaves. The Up Country, on the other hand, was populated by owners of small farms who did not use slaves.

Charles Town was named in honor of King Charles II. At the end of the American Revolution in 1783, the name of the town was changed to Charleston.

I DIDN'T KNOW THAT!

In the early 1600s, King Charles I of England named the region Carolana, which means "land of Charles" in Latin. Later, the name was changed slightly to Carolina.

The early English settlers farmed the land and traded with American Indians. They exchanged items such as guns, tools, and fishhooks for animal skins.

During the 1700s, South Carolinians grew rice and indigo throughout the region. Indigo, a plant that produces a blue dye, was used to color cloth.

The first club for golfers in the United States was created by Scottish settlers in Charleston on September 29, 1786. It was called the South Carolina Golf Club. Club members played on Harleston's Green in Charleston until 1800.

Charles Town established the first free, or public, library in the American colonies in 1698, and the first public museum in 1773.

By 1775, there were about 70,000 people of European descent and 100,000 African Americans living in South Carolina.

Notable People

South Carolinians have contributed to their state, nation, and the world in many ways. Some have advocated tirelessly for the rights of African Americans, women, and children. Others have served their state and their nation as political leaders or military leaders.

ANGELINA GRIMKE (1805–1879)

Angelina Grimke and her older sister Sarah worked tirelessly against slavery and for women's rights. Both sisters were born in Charleston but moved north to Philadelphia because of their strong antislavery beliefs. In 1836, Angelina published a brochure urging women of the South to object to slavery on moral grounds. Both Angelina and Sarah became popular lecturers, attracting thousands to their presentations on the evils of slavery and the need for women to have equal rights.

MARY McLEOD BETHUNE (1875–1955)

Born near Mayesville, Mary McLeod Bethune was one of 17 children of parents who were once slaves. In 1904, she started a school for African American girls in Florida. Although she began with boxes for desks in a run-down house and only five students, she developed the school into a 14-building campus with more than 400 students. Bethune advised presidents Calvin Coolidge, Herbert Hoover, and Franklin D. Roosevelt on the issues of children's health and education, as well as on the rights of African Americans and other minorities.

JAMES BYRNES (1882–1972)

This American statesman served in all three branches of the federal government and was also active in state government. He represented South Carolina in the House of Representatives and in the Senate. After serving as a Supreme Court **justice**, Byrnes advised President Franklin Roosevelt during World War II.

MARION WRIGHT EDELMAN (1939–)

Edelman founded the Children's Defense Fund. This organization's goals include reducing the number of children living in poverty, ensuring that all children have access to education and health care, and reducing abuse and neglect of children. Born in Bennettsville, South Carolina, Edelman was also the first African American woman to become a lawyer in Mississippi.

JESSE JACKSON (1941–)

A political leader, minister, and civil rights activist, Jesse Jackson began working in the civil rights movement in 1966, directing Operation Breadbasket. During the 1970s and 1980s, he expanded his focus, promoting voter registration and political activism as ways to achieve equal rights for all Americans.

James Longstreet (1821–1904) left the U.S. Army when South Carolina seceded from the Union. He then became a brigadier general in the Confederate Army, serving under General Robert E. Lee. He helped lead the Confederate Army to a number of victories. He surrendered with Lee to Union general Ulysses S. Grant in 1865.

Nikki Haley (1972–) was elected the first female governor of South Carolina in 2010. The daughter of immigrants from India, she is also the first nonwhite governor of the state. Haley was first elected to public office as a state representative in 2004.

Population

According to the 2010 U.S. Census, the population of South Carolina is more than 4.6 million. More than two-thirds of the population is made up of people of European descent, and about 28 percent of the population is African American. Over the last 20 years, the number of people of Hispanic descent living in South Carolina has been increasing. Hispanic Americans now make up about 4.5 percent of the population. Most Hispanics in South Carolina trace their roots to Mexico or other parts of Latin America.

South Carolina Population 1950–2010

Over the past two decades, South Carolina's population has grown significantly, by more than 15 percent between 2000 and 2010 alone. What factors might draw people to this state?

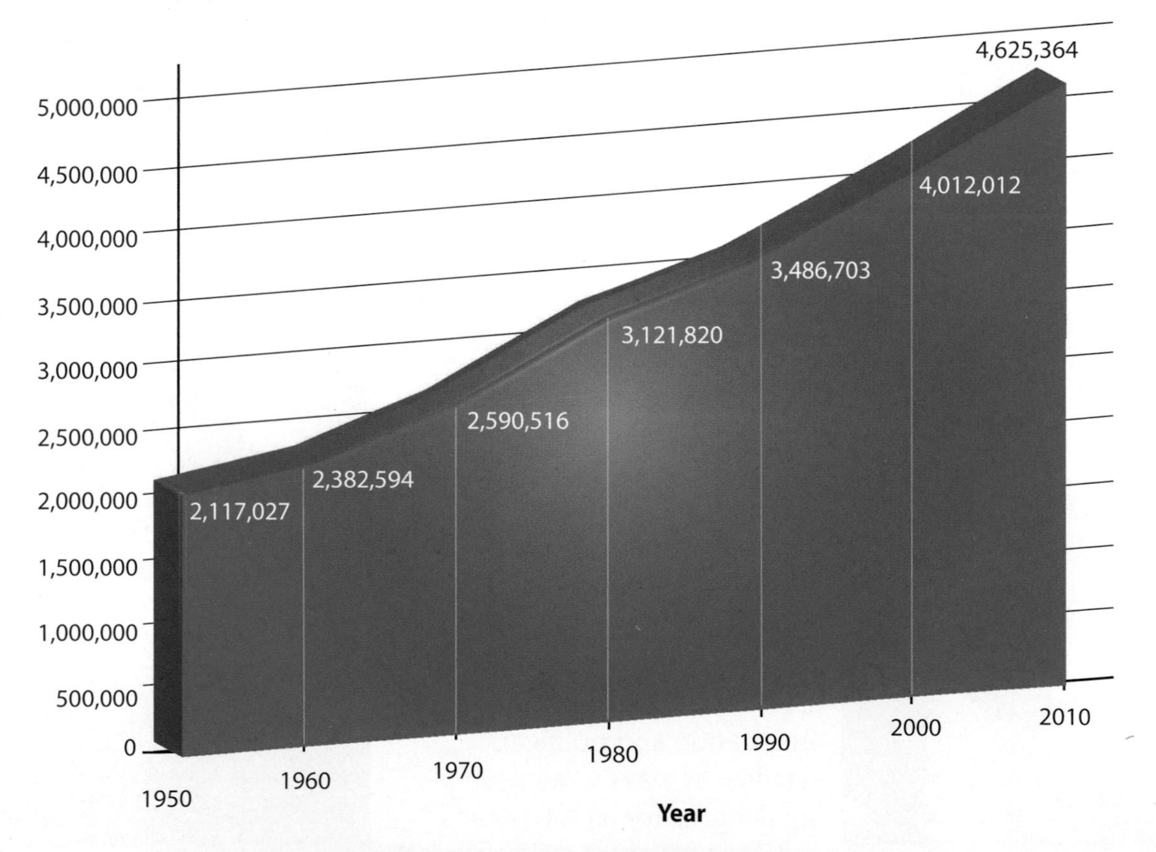

Nearly 14 percent of South Carolinians are age 65 or older, and almost 24 percent of the population is below the age of 18. This age distribution is similar to the national averages. More than three-quarters of the population over the age of 25 has a high school diploma, and about 20 percent of South Carolinians have a college degree. These proportions are below the national averages.

Historically, South Carolina has had a mostly **rural** population. By 2010, more than half of South Carolinians lived in **urban** areas. South Carolina had a population density of 154 people per square mile. This number was significantly higher than the national average of about 87 people per square mile. The largest city in South Carolina was Columbia, with a population of nearly 130,000. Charleston, the second-largest city is home to more than 115,000 people.

Columbia lies along the east bank of the Congaree River, where the Broad and Saluda Rivers join together. With its zoo, historic homes, parks, and rivers, Columbia is a popular place to live in South Carolina.

The five largest cities in South Carolina are Columbia, Charleston, North Charleston, Rock Hill, and Mount Pleasant.

South Carolina has 46 counties. The largest county by area is Horry County.

The average age of South Carolina's residents is increasing at a faster rate than the average age of residents of most other states. This increase is due to more retirees moving to the state than to other states in the nation.

Completed in 1907, the South Carolina State House took 56 years to build. The Senate and the House of Representatives meet in the State House. The governor's offices are also there.

Politics and Government

South Carolina's constitution, which sets forth the way the state is governed, was adopted in 1895. This constitution has been amended extensively since the late 1960s. Like the federal government, the South Carolina government has three branches. They are the executive branch, the legislative, or law-making, branch, and the judicial branch.

The state governor heads the executive branch. The governor may serve two terms. The executive branch includes several other elected officials. The lieutenant governor, secretary of state, attorney general, treasurer, superintendent of education, and commissioner of agriculture are all part of the executive branch.

South Carolina's state legislature is called the General Assembly. It includes a House of Representatives with 124 members and a Senate with 46 members. The judicial branch is the state court system. The highest court is the Supreme Court.

A state-run lottery raises money to support both schools and scholarships in South Carolina.

I DIDN'T KNOW THAT!

One of South Carolina's state songs is called "Carolina on My Mind."

Here is an excerpt from the song.

At the foot hills of the
Appalachian chain,
Down through the rivers,
to the coastal plain,
There's a place that
I call home,
And I'll never be alone,
Singin' this Carolina love song
I've got South Carolina
on my mind
Remembering all those
sunshine Summertimes,
And the Autumns in the
Smokies when the leaves
turn to gold
Touches my heart and thrills
my soul to have South
Carolina on my mind,
With those clean snow-
covered mountain
Wintertimes
And the white sand of the
beaches and those
Carolina peaches,
I've got South Carolina
on my mind.

By the 1680s, people from England, Scotland, and France were immigrating to South Carolina. During the mid-1700s, Germans and Welsh moved to the area.

The Scotch-Irish are people of Scottish origin who lived for a time in the north of Ireland. As land in Ireland grew increasingly expensive, the Scotch-Irish moved to South Carolina during the mid-1700s, drawn by the offer of free land by the colony's government. Some Scotch-Irish also came from Pennsylvania and Virginia.

The government of colonial South Carolina allowed for religious freedom, which encouraged Quakers, Baptists, Presbyterians, and Jews to immigrate to the state. By 1800, Charleston contained one of the largest Jewish populations of any city in the United States.

Many Africans were brought to South Carolina and forced to work as slaves during the 1700s and 1800s. By the late 1800s, three-fifths of the state's people were African American. However, many African Americans left South Carolina, and other areas of the Deep South, from 1916 to 1970. As cotton fields fell to the boll weevil and farming jobs became poorer paid and fewer, better-paying jobs in factories and other businesses drew African Americans to northern urban areas.

The World Grits Festival is held in St. George. This event celebrates grits, an American Indian ground cornmeal dish common in South Carolina and rest of the South.

Today some museums in the state showcase the history and culture of black Americans in South Carolina. The Mann-Simons Cottage in Columbia houses the Museum of African-American Culture. The Avery Research Center for African American History and Culture is in Charleston. Visitors to its museum can see photographs, documents, paintings, and other items about the cultural heritage of African Americans.

The Gullah came from West Africa. They were first brought to work as slaves in the early 17th century. Many Gullah communities in South Carolina were located on small islands and so were separated from the rest of the state. The Gullah's unique culture, included traditional storytelling, special fish and rice dishes, and basket making and other crafts. The term *Gullah* also refers to a distinct language, which is a blend of English and several West African languages. Very few people still speak Gullah. Today communities of Gullah live in the Charleston and Georgetown areas and on Hilton Head and other islands off the South Carolina coast.

After the Civil War, many slaves became sharecroppers. These tenant farmers worked the land in exchange for a share of the crop. If crops were poor or the cost of seeds, tools, and housing were high, they made little money.

The Greenville Scottish Games were created to honor and celebrate the Scotch-Irish in South Carolina. Events include athletic and dancing competitions, as well as craft displays.

Each year Charleston hosts the MOJA Arts Festival, which showcases African American and Caribbean arts. The word *moja* means "one" in Swahili, and the festival emphasizes harmony among the various people in the Charleston community. Its events include a great variety of music, dance, and theater performances, lectures, readings, and arts and crafts exhibits.

The sweetgrass basket, a 1,000-year-old Gullah art form, is still made in the Charleston area. Visitors to Charleston City Market can watch Gullah artisans weaving the baskets with traditional tools made out of bone.

Arts and Entertainment

South Carolina has many notable art museums. The South Carolina State Museum in Columbia has an extensive collection of South Carolina art, as well as other exhibits on history and science. The museum is housed in the historic Columbia Mill, which has been standing since 1893. The Charleston Museum, the United States' first museum, was founded in 1773. Its goal is to preserve and exhibit the cultural and natural history of South Carolina. The Children's Museum of South Carolina, at Myrtle Beach, allows young people to learn by exploring and playing with interactive exhibits.

South Carolina has a long history of theater. The state boasts the nation's first building designed solely for theatrical performances. In 1736, the Dock Street Theatre opened in Charleston. The theater burned down in the fire of 1740, a blaze that destroyed the city's French quarter. A hotel was built on the site in 1809. Much later, in 1937, the building was restored and reopened as the Dock Street Theatre. Today more than 100,000 people attend performances there each year.

Chris Rock often uses his comedy routines to explore race relations and African American poverty. Born in Georgetown, South Carolina, he co-created the popular TV series Everyone Hates Chris, *based on his childhood in Brooklyn, New York.*

Author Pat Conroy was born in Georgia but moved to South Carolina at a young age. In 1972, Conroy published a novel called *The Water Is Wide*. In it, he related his experiences teaching young African American students who were living in poverty. The National Education Association honored Conroy with an award for the book, which was later made into the film *Conrack*. Conroy's best-known novel is *The Prince of Tides*, published in 1986. The novel was made into a film starring Barbra Streisand and Nick Nolte.

Jazz trumpeter and composer Dizzy Gillespie was born in Cheraw in 1917. Along with Charlie Parker, Gillespie is considered to be one of the founders of the bebop movement in jazz. Bebop is a style of jazz based on complex **improvisation** that was developed in the 1940s.

Singer and performer Eartha Kitt was born in North in 1928. When she was young, Kitt toured the world as a dancer with Katherine Dunham's dance troupe. Best known for her work on Broadway, she also acted in a number of television shows and films. Other entertainers born in the state include Chubby Checker, Andie McDowell, and Vanna White.

Comedian Stephen Colbert grew up in Charleston. His show, The Colbert Report, *mocks television news shows. He plays the conceited, conservative host discussing current political issues.*

Mary-Louise Parker has won awards for her acting in the play *Proof* and the television production of *Angels in America*. She was born in Fort Jackson.

Many great writers have come from South Carolina, including DuBose Heyward, James Dickey, and Julia Peterkin. She won the Pulitzer Prize for Literature in 1928.

Nicknamed the "Godfather of Soul" and the "Hardest-Working Man in Show Business," James Brown blended blues, gospel, jazz, and country music into an electrifying sound and stage show. He was born in Barnwell.

Sports

South Carolina's varied landscape and warm climate are perfectly suited to all types of outdoor recreation. With 47 state parks, camping and hiking are year-round activities in South Carolina. Boating, sailing, and swimming are popular in coastal areas. Waterskiing, **parasailing**, canoeing, and kayaking are other water sports that are enjoyed in the state.

South Carolina is one of the premier golfing states in the nation. There are golf courses in every region of the state. The Heritage golf tournament is held each year on Hilton Head Island.

Steeplechase is a popular spectator sport in the state. The Carolina Cup, established in 1930, is hailed as South Carolina's largest sporting event. More than 60,000 fans come to Camden's Springdale Race Course to watch this thrilling sport each year. Spectators come to see Thoroughbred horses racing at 35 miles per hour over 5-foot-high fences.

Born in Silver, South Carolina, Althea Gibson won 11 major tennis titles during the 1950s. She was the first African American player to win the French Open, Wimbledon, and U.S. Open singles championships.

The era of NASCAR speedway racing began at the Darlington Raceway on September 4, 1950. Darlington attracts many visitors to its stock car races. While at the raceway, people can visit the Stock Car Hall of Fame–Joe Weatherly Museum. The museum houses a large collection of historic race cars and driver memorabilia.

College sports, especially football and basketball, are also popular in South Carolina. Although South Carolina does not have any major league professional sports teams, many South Carolinians have played professional sports. Aiken native William Perry, nicknamed the Refrigerator, was a defensive lineman for the Chicago Bears. He was part of the team when it won the National Football League's Super Bowl in 1986. Larry Doby, who was born in Camden, became the first African American athlete to play baseball in the American League in 1947 and the second African American to play in the major leagues.

Wide receiver Roddy White was born on James Island in 1981 and won two state high school wrestling championships. Drafted by the Atlanta Falcons in 2005, he was chosen for the Pro Bowl three times.

I DIDN'T KNOW THAT!

Boxing legend Joe Frazier was born in Beaufort in 1944.

Perhaps the only Major League Baseball player to wear the name of his hometown on his uniform was pitcher Bill Voiselle, from Ninety Six, South Carolina. He wore the number 96 on his jersey.

Shoeless Joe Jackson, born in Brandon Mills, was one of the leading baseball players of the early 20th century.

The United States is a federal republic, consisting of fifty states and the District of Columbia. Alaska and Hawai'i are the only non-contiguous, or non-touching, states in the nation. Today, the United States of America is the third-largest country in the world in population. The United States Census Bureau takes a census, or count of all the people, every ten years. It also regularly collects other kinds of data about the population and the economy. How does South Carolina compare to the national average?

Comparison Chart

United States 2010 Census Data *	USA	South Carolina
Admission to Union	NA	May 23, 1788
Land Area (in square miles)	3,537,438.44	30,109.47
Population Total	308,745,538	4,625,364
Population Density (people per square mile)	87.28	153.62
Population Percentage Change (April 1, 2000, to April 1, 2010)	9.7%	15.3%
White Persons (percent)	72.4%	66.2%
Black Persons (percent)	12.6%	27.9%
American Indian and Alaska Native Persons (percent)	0.9%	0.4%
Asian Persons (percent)	4.8%	1.3%
Native Hawaiian and Other Pacific Islander Persons (percent)	0.2%	0.1%
Some Other Race (percent)	6.2%	2.5%
Persons Reporting Two or More Races (percent)	2.9%	1.7%
Persons of Hispanic or Latino Origin (percent)	16.3%	5.1%
Not of Hispanic or Latino Origin (percent)	83.7%	94.9%
Median Household Income	$52,029	$44,695
Percentage of People Age 25 or Over Who Have Graduated from High School	80.4%	76.3%

*All figures are based on the 2010 United States Census, with the exception of the last two items. Percentages may not add to 100 because of rounding.

How to Improve My Community

Strong communities make strong states. Think about what features are important in your community. What do you value? Education? Health? Forests? Safety? Beautiful spaces? Government works to help citizens create ideal living conditions that are fair to all by providing services in communities. Consider what changes you could make in your community. How would they improve your state as a whole? Using this concept web as a guide, write a report that outlines the features you think are most important in your community and what improvements could be made. A strong state needs strong communities.

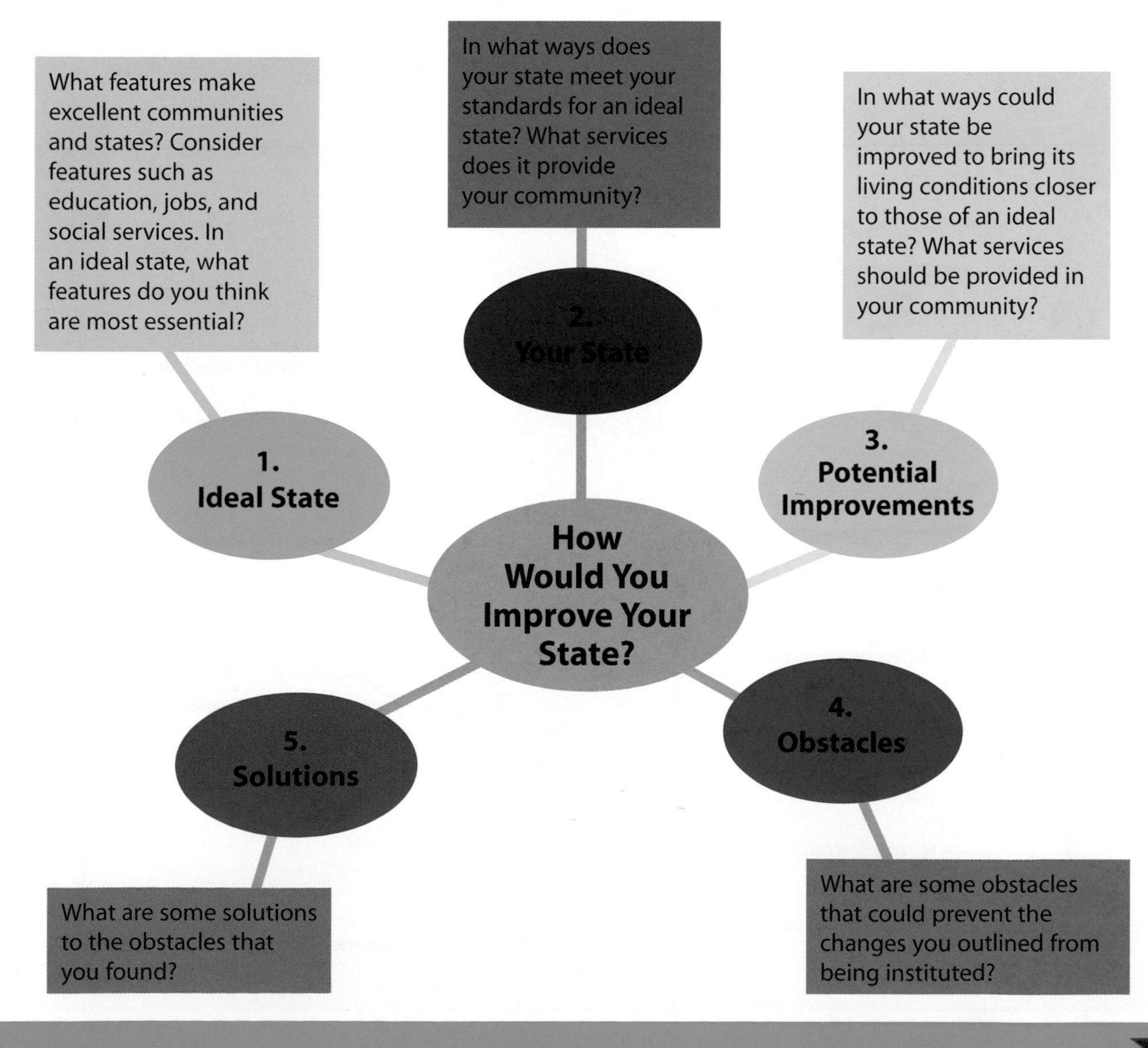

Think about these questions and then use your research skills to find the answers and learn more fascinating facts about South Carolina. A teacher, librarian, or parent may be able to help you locate the best sources to use in your research.

1

What is the official state dance of South Carolina?

a. The hustle
b. The shag
c. The waltz
d. The square dance

2

What interesting structure is found at Huntington Beach State Park?

3

Which South Carolina native was killed in 1986 when the space shuttle *Challenger* exploded?

4

What is the state song of South Carolina?

a. "South Carolina on My Mind"
b. "Carolina"
c. "Sweet Home Carolina"
d. "My Carolina"

5

Where in South Carolina did the first battle in the Civil War take place?

a. Columbia
b. Fort Moultrie
c. Fort Sumter
d. Port Royal

6

Which state grows more peaches than South Carolina?

a. California
b. Florida
c. Arizona
d. North Carolina

7

Which of the following competitions are held at the annual Sun Fun Festival at Myrtle Beach in South Carolina:

a. Bubble-gum blowing contest
b. Watermelon-eating contest
c. Sandcastle-building contest
d. All of the above

8

Which of the following civil rights leaders was from South Carolina?

a. Jesse Jackson
b. Martin Luther King, Jr.
c. Malcolm X

erosion: the wearing away of rock and soil

improvisation: a performance done without previous preparation

justice: a judge in a court of law

parasailing: the sport of soaring in the air while harnessed to a parachute that is attached to a moving motorboat

patents: exclusive rights granted to inventors or companies to manufacture and sell their inventions

persecution: the act of continually treating someone in a harmful or cruel way, or being treated that way, especially because of one's beliefs or one's heritage

plantations: large estates where crops are grown

rural: of, or living in, the country

secede: to formally withdraw

steeplechase: a horse race on a course with artificial ditches, fences, and other obstacles over which the horses must jump

urban: of, or living in, the city

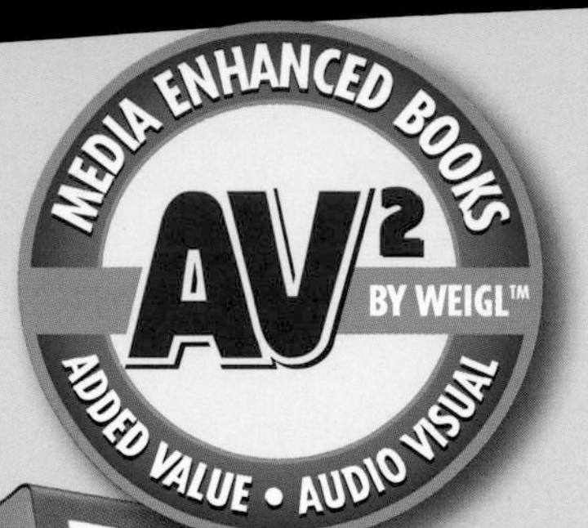

Log on to www.av2books.com

AV² by Weigl brings you media enhanced books that support active learning. Go to www.av2books.com, and enter the special code found on page 2 of this book. You will gain access to enriched and enhanced content that supplements and complements this book. Content includes video, audio, web links, quizzes, a slide show, and activities.

Audio
Listen to sections of the book read aloud.

Video
Watch informative video clips.

Embedded Weblinks
Gain additional information for research.

Try This!
Complete activities and hands-on experiments.

WHAT'S ONLINE?

Try This!

Test your knowledge of the state in a mapping activity.

Find out more about precipitation in your city.

Plan what attractions you would like to visit in the state.

Learn more about the early natural resources of the state.

Write a biography about a notable resident of South Carolina.

Complete an educational census activity.

Embedded Weblinks

Discover more attractions in South Carolina.

Learn more about the history of the state.

Learn the full lyrics of the state song.

Video

Watch a video introduction to South Carolina.

Watch a video about the features of the state.

EXTRA FEATURES

Audio
Listen to sections of the book read aloud.

Key Words
Study vocabulary, and complete a matching word activity.

Slide Show
View images and captions, and prepare a presentation.

Quizzes
Test your knowledge.

AV² was built to bridge the gap between print and digital. We encourage you to tell us what you like and what you want to see in the future.

Sign up to be an AV² Ambassador at www.av2books.com/ambassador.

Due to the dynamic nature of the Internet, some of the URLs and activities provided as part of AV² by Weigl may have changed or ceased to exist. AV² by Weigl accepts no responsibility for any such changes. All media enhanced books are regularly monitored to update addresses and sites in a timely manner. Contact AV² by Weigl at 1-866-649-3445 or av2books@weigl.com with any questions, comments, or feedback.